First edition 2019
Second edition 2023

With historic thanks to Danica Ognjenovic, Graham Wrathmell and Jeremy Hall.
With specific thanks to Tony Herbert, Chrissy Collinson, Paul Collinson, Brian Lewis, Ben, Ellie and others.

Masthead Typeface: Blakely
Bodytext Typeface: Bodoni 72
Originally published by 21st Century Publications B98 7LG (www.21stcenturyprint.com)
This edition published through mixam.co.uk

About the author: Vic Allen was born in Hipperholme; was educated in both public schools and comprehensive schools; went to Canterbury University; worked as a journalist in London for 15 years; edited Yorkshire's Artscene magazine for 15 years; was artistic director of Dean Clough in Halifax for 15 years, and was executive director of an arts charity (ACDC) for five years. He had planned to do the latter for 15 years, but was diagnosed with Myeloma in 2022 and is currently redundant. Vic has been instructed to take the DVLC's 'Speed Awareness' course three times.

MONUMENTAL OVERSIGHTS

PUBLIC SCULPTURES IN YORKSHIRE

by Vic Allen

PREFACE *by Vic Allen*

I am no expert. There are, here, few original facts and probably much that is dubious. But in this, the year of 'Yorkshire Sculpture International', somebody had to pay heed to the monuments that local communities variously butter with myths or (contrariwise) blithely ignore. While I run an art gallery, there was neither time nor money to commission a 'proper' photographer (let alone a 'proper' writer) but I am, at least, an authentic sciolist. Oh. And the idea behind *Monumental Oversights* is one that I've long cherished.

I could say it began with my father. He it was that first told me the story of Halifax's Thorneycroft horse. When after his death I learned the truth about the horse, I was struck by the way that despite the evidence of our eyes we can be so easily lulled and gulled by a consensus.

But no less influential was the chance remark of the sculptor, Michael Sandle. In 2008 he had generously enabled the Dean Clough Galleries to exhibit a large work from the Tate Collection[1] and it seemed that the least we could do was to drive him back to Leeds station to collect the London train.

As we crawled into City Square, Sandle remarked how he was always glad to admire anew the statue there of the Black Prince. I agreed wholeheartedly. You don't argue when an internationally renowned artist expresses an opinion. The statue on its plinth is, what, seven... eight metres high? It weighs an estimated 20 tonnes; it was actually brought to Leeds from Hull by barge because overland transport in 1890 would have been impossible.

Yet, despite knowing Leeds for over 45 years, I had never consciously noticed the bloody thing before then.

I had considered basing this exploration of public sculptures in Yorkshire on the works that were most favoured by artists. But after asking several artists it soon became clear that most of them were as oblivious to public sculpture as I had been to the Black Prince. It wasn't just that they had no preferences. Beside the standard totems (you know the sort of thing: Michelangelo's 'David', Rodin's 'Thinker', Jagger's war memorial...) some of them could not casually recall a single regional sculpture. Which shocked me.

A few months ago a national curator visited Dean Clough Mills with a view to mounting a sculptural exhibition in a top floor space that is poised for development. She declined it almost at once on the grounds that it wasn't environmentally controlled. It seems that the term 'sculpture' now embraces anything that is three dimensional, including the type of installations that the critic Herbert Read , bless him, would have dismissed as 'assemblage'. This shocked me, too.

I mean, I didn't spill my Pimms or crush my green carnation in a panic. If you work in the arts (as distinct from teaching the arts) you tend not to get hung up on definitions. They don't help. But both these events suggest that the 'opinion formers' in the arts are not so much broadening definitions as denying public sculpture the right to any kind of aesthetic status. They don't abjure the public realm; they just want to control it.

Outside the Henry Moore Institute in Leeds is a tree with a stone pillar next to it. It's a shard from Joseph Beuys's 1982 project called '7,000 Oaks'. As bids to raise environmental consciousness went, '7,000 Oaks' was a fairly low-key scheme. A decent *Blue Peter* TV campaign would have generated far more boscage. Beuys's plan to "extend the gallery into the city" is less a bid to include the public in the arts, than a licence for aesthetes to laud their superior insight in the streets.

The idea that a lump of basalt next to a tree establishes the concept that an oak 'can be a sculpture' is frankly risible; the moronic notion of a class in thrall to a rudderless sophistication. There is, though, at least here a recognition that a public sculpture is a consensual object. Sculptures are probably the closest that high-art gets to the public realm and, like TV programmes, they can succeed both famously and infamously. Only if they are indifferent do they fail.

It is in this spirit that *Monumental Oversights* has been mounted. It is not comprehensive. At all. A survey of public monuments by members of Sheffield Hallam

University enumerated over 300 of them[3] in Sheffield alone. In order to retain a little focus I took an early decision to exclude war memorials, animal statues and shrines. I was also consciously prejudiced against Queen Victorias, corporate statues and obvious high-art statements. These last tend to de-laminate themselves from public life, although there are exceptions. Probably not in the case of the dumpy monarchs, but Harrogate's Victoria Centre and Darlington's 'Train' are included here. I don't think Bradford's Delius monument, the giant mesh packhorse in Leeds Trinity Centre, or the gift-shoppy seagulls at No. 1 City Square have yet 'found their public'.

I excluded the rash of sculpture-studded country parks in mid-Yorkshire. The Yorkshire Sculpture Park itself does fine work, of course, but so far as the public realm goes it has the culture of an airport. Which is to say it's clean, shiny and functional except when it's being updated (i.e. always); while the only souls with a true sense of ownership are (to sustain the simile) the airport staff and a few sad enthusiasts who on rainy days sit in their cars at the end of the runway...

Hmm. Airports. It would have been good to snap the 'Robin Hood' statue at his eponymous airport; I was annoyed to miss the 'Seated Man' at Castleton Rigg (although Sean Henry might be glad that I did); I felt guilty passing over Thirsk's statue of 'James Herriot', and still don't understand why I didn't pin down Quentin Bell's 'Levitating Woman' in Leeds.

I'd love to have asked at least one farmer about the onus of unofficially tending neolithic monuments that were thoughtlessly discarded in their fields, or to have asked one of the tenants in the Waterside Centre how they felt when they opened their windows every morning to the sight of two figures frozen in perpetual coitus. Maybe next time[4].

A modesty pill that has to be publicly swallowed (if only because it is obvious to all) is to stress that this book could not have been compiled so quickly without the internet and, in particular, local paper websites. The internet nurses its fair share of mumpsimuses (i.e. cherished and indissoluble errors); but I soon recognised this as a satisfying analogue for the tendency of the public realm to generate unsubstantiated myths about its statues.

Nor should we believe those traditionalists who tell us that such errors would not have happened in the days when books were the main information source. One of the silliest errors you'll ever find is Michelangelo's statue of Moses in the church of San Pietro in Vicoli. He has horns on his head. Like a goat. Moses was always represented this way because a difficult Hebrew passage in the bible described him as coming down from Mount Sinai with 'horns' about his bonce, by which it was probably meant beams of light. 783,137 words to translate and you get ONE wrong, eh?

So what, in the end, is this amateur, error-laden and partial book (and photographic exhibition) about? There's a delightful forum exchange on the 'Secret Leeds' web-site[6] about the Black Prince statue (i.e. the one I ignored for 45 years). The basic facts about the statue ("*new city status*", "*industrialist funding*", "*barge*", "*cheering crowds*", *yada-yada...*) reappear, before someone offers a highly informed and therefore distinctly tenuous rationale for the swarthy aristocrat, thus:

'The Black Prince' was chosen to symbolise chivalry, good government, patronage of the arts and education, encouragement of industry, and democratic values; the names of men from the prince's era entwining the pedestal emphasise the allegory. Sir John Chandos (founder member of the Order of the Garter); Walter de Mannay (soldier); Bertram du Guesclin (military leader); Chaucer (father of English literature); Van Artevelde (encouraged Flemish weavers and dyers to visit northern England, laying the foundations of the textile industry); William of Wykham (Lord Chancellor, Bishop of Winchester, endowed Winchester College, and New College, Oxford, member of the Good Parliament) etc. etc..

Immediately after this peroration comes this less exalt-able post:–

"It used to be said that the statue of the Black Prince had been placed in City Square, near the station, pointing South to tell all the southerners who've just got off the train to b****r off back down south!"

'Monumental Oversights' lies somewhere between these two mindsets. It's about the disputed sense of ownership that a sculpture attracts. It's about the fallibility of the sculptors – all of whom I admire enormously. It takes brass balls as much as bronze ingots to be a public sculptor. They have no option but to be exposed. Theirs is no safe gallery environment, where opinion is mediated by *politesse* and where private thoughts are only exchanged in the car on the way home.

It's about the fallibility of vandals (none of whom offered my camera a statue with a traffic cone on its head) and of the various Town, City and Borough Councils who have 'dropped clangers' over the years... although it needs to be emphasised that the latter are too frequently scapegoated for, erm, 'monumental errors'. Most monuments are, after all, generated by groups and organisations other than 'the bloody Council'.

There's a thesis to be written (and probably has been several times) about the oscillating influence of public committees, village groups, commerce, churches, the Arts Council etc. on the choice and frequency of public installations. An article in the *Guardian* in 2009 saw the editor of the *Burlington Magazine* sounding off on the topic: "Every town has now got to have the local celebrity. Fine. We used to do it with blue plaques. But now you've got to have a bloody great bronze. They're not artistic – occasionally competent is about all you can say".

What would 'Burlington Man' make of the current sculptural tendency to brash giant-ism – which surely reflects a collusion of interests by tourist board quangos, regional egotism and novelty-seeking day-trippers?

But ultimately this book is about the primordial fallibility, namely ignorance[7]. No expert (as I have confessed), I should not have dared attempt this topic if it wasn't less a consideration of statues than of the public realm. Because within the public realm all observations are valid; it's only conclusions that are pompous – and I'm not offering any.

Halifax, West Yorkshire 2019

ABOUT THE PHOTOGRAPHY...

If anyone looked at the frontispiece picture and thought it was 'great', well it's actually a rather dull picture that has simply been injected with Photoshop® steroids. Zoom lenses, deviously sensitive sensors and ever more clever 'in-camera software' have made bad photographs increasingly hard to take; but they've made honest photographs increasingly hard to take, as well.

No self-conscious creature was ever honest, of course; but I did want to present the statues here without the usual visual fireworks of dizzying verticals, bokeh impressionism and noses that were as expansive as African savannahs. This meant accuracy and detail; which is to say high-class optics and the digital equivalent of a medium format camera.

Which were both well beyond my means.

The compromise was a curious beast called the Sigma Quattro DP3. This uses a novel technology that sounds like something from *Star Trek* ('the Foveon chip') and has a 70mm equivalent prime lens (as distinct from a zoom lens) that is both sharp and – crucially – virtually free of distortion.

Most camera journalists despise the Quattro. They have a point. It is a pig of a camera to use. As if a prime lens wasn't frustrating enough, it's a camera that is always hungry for more light, which wants a tripod most of the time, and (since it lacks a viewfinder) is a nightmare to use on a sunny day.

Then again, as any one involved in husbandry (let alone parenthood) would confirm, it's usually the neediest bird in the nest that becomes the most loved. But enough of this geekery[8]...

PREFACE TO THE SECOND EDITION

Why produce a second edition of this book?

1. The first edition sold out.

2. The subject is still topical. Indeed public sculpture became all the rage in 2020. And I mean rage. In the USA, for instance, the removal of Confederate monuments gathered apace after the murder of George Floyd. In the UK the merchant and philanthropist Edward Colston (1636-1721) had his statue toppled and dumped in Bristol docks by a mob who objected that his fortune had largely come from the sale of shares that he held in a slave trading business. A similar controversy occurred in Oxford, where Henry Alfred Pegram's (1862-1937) statue of the 'colonialist' Cecil Rhodes was arguably spared violence due to its lofty emplacement in Oriel College. Edward Colston's statue was later salvaged and put on supine display – still damaged and scarred with graffiti – in Bristol's M Shed. The 'honour of a statue', argued the Bristol protesters, "...should be reserved for those who bring about positive change and who fight for peace, equality and social unity". Were this admirable sentiment to be retrospectively enforced it is certain that this book would be a lot thinner. A case in point might be the glistering Hull statue of William of Orange – who, it turns out, was the man who actually bought Colston's shares in the Royal African Company.

3. This second edition enables me to commemorate Tony Herbert, who assisted immeasurably with the first edition of 'Monumental Oversights' and who prematurely died in 2020. Tony had a gyroscopic spirit; the kind of person whose loss leaves the lives of everyone who knew them permanently off-kilter. I hope any readers have been or will be lucky enough to know such a soul.

4. It also gives me a chance to thank Steve McClarence for his delightfully written feature in the *Yorkshire Post* (...a remarkable newspaper whose right-wing soul is ever-troubled – rightly but rewardingly so – by its communal remit).

5. A second edition means that I can amend a screaming 'literal' in the first edition which I allow myself to think nobody spotted. It was the kind of mistake that makes the internal organs of writers regelate and induces much nocturnal gnawing of pillows. For what it's worth, my favourite ever 'literal' was a listing for a christmas show called *'Postman Pat: Where's Jess?'* which my fat fingers converted to *'Postman Pat: Where's Jesus?'*. It is quite possible, of course, that the error in the first edition was widely noticed and that people were simply too embarrassed to mention it to me. If so, accept my gratitude and do please maintain your discretion.

6. Notwithstanding 'literals', I have left most of the original text unaltered. This is a topical, not an academic, book and it should be allowed to 'date'. That said, a second preface means I can at least mention my belated discovery that the Huddersfield statue of Harold Wilson in St. George's Square replaced a contrastingly imperious, nine feet tall statue of Robert Peel. The latter was sculpted out of Sicilian marble by William Theed (1804–91) and persisted from 1873 to 1949 before it crumbled in the moist, acidic air of the times.

7. I might also add to the above a claim passed on to me by someone involved in the construction of Harrogate's Victoria Centre who swore blind that the figurines on its palisade were designed by the architect's wife. I could try and validate this claim but – look – you need to grasp now the concept of this book, which is to actively celebrate the rumours that swirl around the all too solid flesh of its ostensible topic.

Farnley, North Yorkshire 2023

The Devil's Arrows • Boroughbridge

"Borobrigg keep out o' way, for Aldborough town I will ding down!" ... is what the Devil is supposed to have shouted from Howe Hill as he threw these stones (for reasons unrecorded) at Aldborough. He missed by a mile.

There were originally four stones (five if you credit Wikipedia, seven if you credit a 17th C. peripatetic angler[1]). One was recorded as lying prone at the end of the 16th C. and later broken up for a bridge (attributed by folklore to John Metcalfe[2]) over the nearby River Tutt.

Archaeologists associate the Devil's Arrows (also known as the 'Three Sisters' and, bizarrely, the 'Three Greyhounds'[3]) with an extensive complex of nearby barrows and

henges. It's reckoned that 50,000 standing stones were erected in neolithic Europe. No one really knows why... so the myths go about their folksy business untrammelled.

There are tales of sacrifices in which blood ran down the runnels in the millstone grit. Another tale claims the devil tried to hang his grandmother from the stones and she kicked the runnels out with her heels. You can ask Old Nick the truth of this yourself by walking round the stones twelve times at midnight. Or you can put the grooves down to weathering.

At 6.9m high the southernmost menhir (in the grounds of a private house) is the second-largest in England. To get the photograph on the left you have to climb up a tree. To get the photograph below you have to stand in horse droppings and stable sweepings.

Said to have been dragged from Plumpton Rocks[4], the local farmer obviously affords the menhirs considerable respect – which is more than can be said for the traffic on the A1 and for the speculative builders in the next field.

THE PRINCE CONSORT • HALIFAX

"When Queen Victoria unveiled this statue it was greeted, not with the expected cheers, but with a stunned silence, followed by gasps of dismay. The sculptor had made a gross error in the depiction of the horse. Such was his shame that the next day he committed suicide."[1]

This story is so often corrected that its persistence in Halifax is a testament to the communal appetite for myth; especially so, as the report above refers to a near identical statue *(bottom right)*[2] by the same sculptor that was erected in 1866 in Wolverhampton.

Thomas Thorneycroft had drawn Albert's horse, 'Nimrod', prior to the prince's death and was responsible for a third statue in Liverpool at about the same time *(bottom left)*[3]. Evidently this was also rumoured to have "inaccuracies both in the horse's anatomy and in the Prince's riding posture"[4], although the suicide story is not repeated.

The Halifax statue (16 foot high and weighing 1.5 tons) was moved to Sparrow Park in 1900. It was originally centrally located and a contemporary report has 10,000 people attending its unveiling by Sir Francis Crossley (then MP for the West Riding). Notably, the report continued...

"The figure of the prince is bareheaded. He is seated in a dignified manner and represented as being in the act of receiving

public honour, having a scroll in one hand and the bridle in the other. Over a frock coat he wears the order of the Garter with its star. The horse is a highly bred outstripping charger, and is a graceful work of artistic skill, being modelled from an animal often ridden by the Prince".

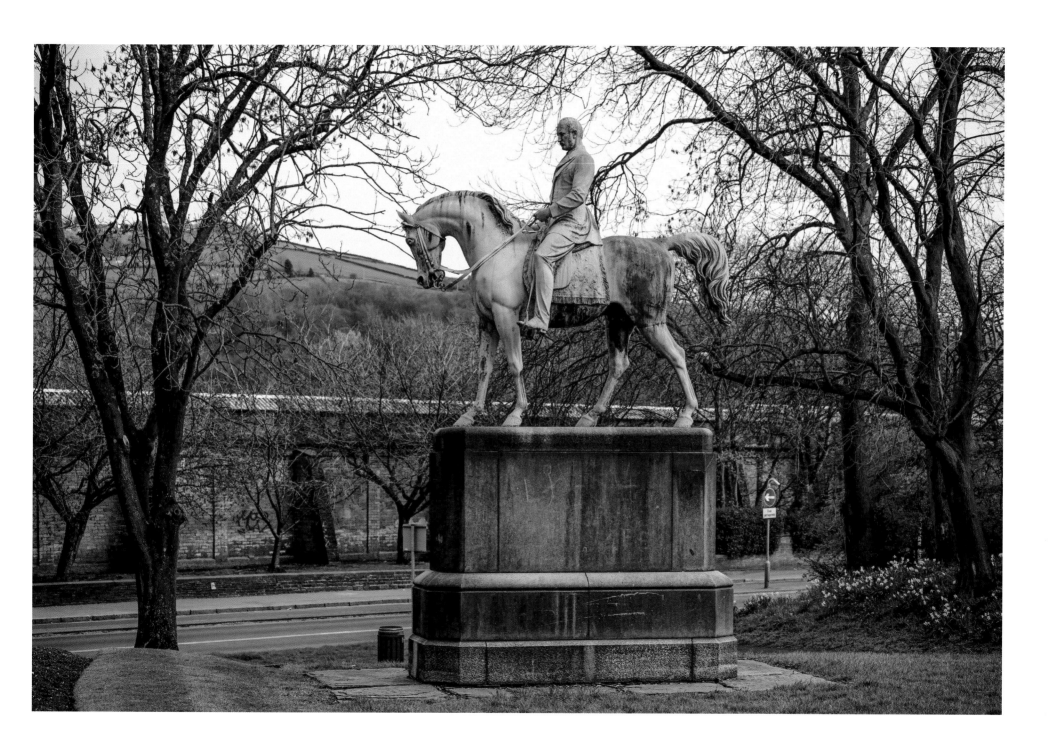

King Billy • Hull

In the 'Glorious Revolution' of 1688, Hull declared early for King William of Orange who went on to depose the Catholic King James II. William was the last person to successfully invade England and the King who first acceded to the Bill of Rights – whose libertarian freedoms probably appealed more to the city's mercantile interests than to its egalitarian principles.

Putting aside the fable that 'King Billy' dismounts and pops into the proximitous but currently vacant pub at midnight; the local legend is that the renowned sculptor, Peter Scheemakers (who has 15 works in Westminster Abbey alone), committed suicide after the statue was erected and it was realised that he had 'forgotten' the stirrups.

As with Thorneycroft's supposed suicide in Halifax, the dates hardly bear this out. The statue was erected by public subscription at a cost of £785 in 1734 and gilded in 1768. The King is posturing as Caesar. The omission of stirrups (a Chinese invention not adopted in the west until Mediaeval times) is deliberate. A famous Jacobite toast[1] recounts how William III died of complications after falling when his horse stumbled on a molehill. The choice of an equestrian statue, erected over 30 years after his death, seems more insensitive than locating that toilet under his feet...

Thomas Chippendale • Otley

Just as Peter Scheemakers' bust of Shakespeare in Westminster Abbey was iconised on £20 notes[1], so the 300th birth anniversary of Thomas Chippendale gave a brief celebrity to the mien of the bronze statue outside the Elizabethan Grammar School building in Otley's Clapgate. The irony being that there are no contemporary likenesses[2] of either gentleman (Albert Hodge's 1906 Chippendale sculpture outside the V&A is also fictitious).

It is not certain that Chippendale attended the grammar school or that he was born in (rather than near) Otley; but it is known that his dad came from Cleckheaton. The 1987 monument was proposed by the Sam Chippindale Foundation[3]. It was 'fenced in' for commercial purposes in 2005 (the school is now a restaurant) and has latterly become buried in urban furniture. If you want a 'quiet' picture you have to take it at midnight *(left)*.

The statue is in the early, loose style of Barnsley sculptor Graham Ibbeson. The Rococo interior designer proffers a splat back with a slight stoop – the consequence of his 'cabriole leg' (knee out, ankle in!). Such glum humility seems apt for a man who struggled all his life with the tardy payments of an elite who now affect to celebrate him. But whose face was it? We asked the sculptor. "It's based on a friend," Ibbeson said affably. "My wife's brother. Colin Greenwood. It's a good English name!". You read it here, first...

THE VICTORIA CENTRE • HARROGATE

Harrogate's Victoria Centre opened in November 1992. Its owners, Coal Pension Properties, spent £50m. on a design that is said to have been inspired by Andrea Palladio's 16th C. basilica at Vicenza – a building studded with an array of classical figurines on its balustrades.

The mall replaced a long-established market hall and was probably destined to generate a modicum of resentment. This was unexpectedly augmented in 1995 when the populist writer, Bill Bryson, reserved its "Georgian/Italianate/fuck-knows style" for sustained invective in his travelogue, *'Notes from a Small Island'*.

The mall was, he said, "...heartbreakingly awful, the worst kind of pastiche architecture – a sort of Bath Crescent meets Crystal Palace with a roof by B&Q".

It seems unlikely, though, that Bryson would *truly* have preferred the ubiquitous 'tin shed' and quite likely that the American's jibe would have faded – were it not for the plaster statues. Sporting expressions that you only find in Ladybird Books, the rooftop figurines recall a pre-digital age when architects and planners enlivened their plans with 'architecturally fulfilled' Letraset figures.

"... it looks as if two dozen citizens of various ages are about to commit suicide" Bryson memorably quipped.

There are, in fact, only five mouldings (including a family group) – which is an economy whose repetition radiates contempt for any would-be admirers. Even so, the town enjoyed the joke when during cleaning work in December 2005 they were wrapped in hats and scarves donated by a commercial tenant to 'ward off the cold'.

The statues are said to represent the mall's customers and staff. And while the unidentified sculptor might be excused for failing to distinguish between the employees of HMV and TK-Maxx, it seems fair to object that the Harrogate public *(see picture below, taken on Easter Day)* are capable of being more distinctive than he/she credits.

ORPHEUS • HAREWOOD HOUSE

Astrid Zidower's 'Orpheus' statue on the terrace of Harewood House replaced a frost-damaged fountain in 1984.

According to Zidower's biographer[1] it was Lincoln Kirstein, the founder of the American Ballet School, who suggested the work as he owned one of the five original 12-inch figurines on which it is based. However, in a letter to *The Independent*, the late Earl of Harewood maintained it was a mutual friend, the critic Richard Buckle.

"Zidower told me it was the hardest thing she had ever done because of its immense size," wrote the Earl.

Zidower was a war time refugee; a German Jew adopted by a Quaker family in Sheffield. She attended the RCA in 1952 and enjoyed a career featuring national commissions and rock star connections. Her Orpheus (whose face – at least! – belongs to a supposed 60's pop star) seems to predate the liaison with Eurydice and to invoke earlier myths about his ability to charm animals with his lyre. But while there are ancient mosaics and even a few latter-day paintings[2] that feature leopards it is hard to find a specific reference for the stark pose. There's nothing in Gluck or Stravinsky, let alone Rilke[3] or Sydney Goodsir Smith[4] that offers explanation.

BILLY BREMNER • LEEDS

It's a shrine, really. A painted statue adorned with items of pilgrimage, surrounded by a regiment of memorial plaques. Billy Bremner captained Leeds United F.C. during its most successful period.

With its Apollonian, bronzed hair and toothy smile Bremner's statue stands outside Elland Road in a boxing pose, looking like a cross between a Balkan 'turbo sculpture' and Miffy from the Bash Street Kids; a remark prompted not out of spite but because the red-haired Scot actually had a reasonably noble profile.

The pose is derived from a *Daily Mail* photograph captured during a moderately significant 1972 match against Arsenal F.C. and it's tempting to conclude that the distortion of the angled lens was not taken into account.

The sculpture is the work of Frances Segelman (b.1949), a Leeds born artist renowned for royal and celebrity bronzes. When unveiled in 1999 the bronze Bremner was unpainted but during 'renovation' in 2010 he assumed white paint and – initially – red hair.

It was Goethe who observed, "people of refinement avoid vivid colours". It seems typically vulgar of football fans to select Bremner's statue for adoration and to eschew Graham Ibbeson's immaculately

unpainted, 2012 statue of Don Revie *(bottom right)*... the manager of Leeds United during Bremner's captaincy looks on from the sidelines, much as he did in life.

That being said, Goethe's colour-theory was always flawed – while *anyone* who watches BBC4 will know that classical sculptures were almost invariably painted ('polychromatic' is the academically preferred term). It's just that there persists a kind of consensual amnesia about the fact.

There is still a tendency to think, for instance, that the colouring on ancient Egyptian sculptures betokens a cultural crudity rather than to consider the preservative effect of the sand that they were buried in.

And while modern science has provided more detailed evidence, it has been known definitively that Classical statues were coloured since the end of the 19th Century; not that this knowledge stopped 'experts' in the 1930s from polishing the Elgin marbles to an opalescent shine.

There is, it has been suggested, an inherent racism in this monotonous prejudice; a reluctance, for instance, to recognise the ethnic diversity of the Roman Empire.

But while one shouldn't read too much into remarks such as "the whiter the body is, the more beautiful it is" by seminal

aesthetes such as Johan Wincklemann (1717–68), it seems obvious that the modern emphasis on 'form' owes a great deal to this misinterpretation of archaeological sculpture.

It's an unthinking prejudice that persists among most UK artists and there's a snide joy in the notion that Leeds's football fans are in this instance ahead of the game...

J.B. PRIESTLEY • BRADFORD

It seems odd that sculptor Ian Judd didn't receive more commissions on the strength of his J.B.Priestley . The author's expression is convincing, the detail judicious and the stance credible – even if the Media Museum staff used to joke about him 'farting into his coat'. Judd's studio was in Halifax's Dean Clough mill for many years and Priestley's polystyrene maquette still lurks in the building's corridors.

Since 1986 the windy old hypocrite has looked out over the town he chose to define him ('Bruddersford'), as delighted as any 'fellow traveller' could be to be raised above Queen Victoria's nearby monument. You almost get the impression he's stood there for his own benefit. You can't see his boots without a cherry picker, for instance, and

it's satisfying to imagine he might be wearing open-toed sandals or maybe vans.

A photographer bent on novelty can align Priestley's pipe with an air conditioning vent on the Pictureville roof so that on cold days it looks stoked; but truly the best angle to catch is the intended one, which is perhaps evidence of a well-sited monument.

Two people watched as I wrestled with my tripod: a lad whose blotched face hinted at a drug-impeded circulation and an elderly gentleman in a shalwar kameez carrying what I assumed was a quran. Unexpectedly it was the latter who spat suddenly: "You're in the garden you fucking git!".

He went on to display a command of English invective that Norman Tebbit would surely have applauded and which illustrated that any religious mania he bore was superseded by his Tourettes. The lad, meanwhile, waited until I telescoped the tripod away before asking, gently: "Is that camera worth much?". Bradford never disappoints.

MATTHEW WILSON • SKIPTON

The Wilsons of Eshton Hall, nr. Gargrave had a motto: "Whenever Craven calls, a Wilson will be ready". They know what's best for us. *They* wouldn't burden us with a plebiscite. Even so, they might be waiting a while for that call. Sir Matthew has stood on Skipton high street for 131 years, yet nobody I spoke to knew anything about him.

It turns out that Sir Matthew is one of the people who actually "read the riot act". Athwart the Town Hall steps in 1842, he commanded the 'Plug Rioters' to disperse. They didn't and the 'Anna Fields Fight' (in which a soldier died) was the result.

A Justice of the Peace at 22, Sir Matthew became a liberal M.P. but managed only short tenures of seat. His longest tenure, celebrated on his plinth, was as M.P. for West Yorkshire North. His relative, Frances Mary Richardson Currer, seems in retrospect a more deserving choice for a memorial. She had a reputation for generosity and created one of the largest libraries in the early 19th century.

The pioneer of women's education, Lucy Cavendish (1841–1925) refers to Wilson "pegging away with his usual spirit" at the hustings once, when Gladstone appeared and stole his audience. It seems pertinent then that Wilson's substantial and expensive statue was the work of Albert Bruce-Joy, a Dublin born sculptor who had made the Gladstone statue outside Bow Church in 1882.

Sir Matthew Wilson, Baronet (1802–1891) • Sculpted by Albert Bruce-Joy (1842–1924)

SIR MATTHEW WILSON BARONET

M.P. FOR THE WEST RIDING OF YORKSHIRE, NORTHERN DIVISION 1874 TO 1885.

FIRST M.P. FOR THE SKIPTON DIVISION OF YORKSHIRE 1885 — 1885.

Richard Cobden • Bradford

Your true Bradfordians are usually well aware that among the 35 rulers of England that are embedded in the City Hall walls is a comparatively rare[1] statue of Oliver Cromwell. He poses in an unexpectedly florid hat between the man he beheaded and the man who dug up his supposed remains three years after his death and had them hanged, decapitated and dumped in a Tyburn pit.

Bradford was Parliamentarian during the civil war. It repeatedly changed hands but the history is hardly relevant. The booming industrial town that in 1873 was happy to pay £63 for each of its stone monarchs would have given little heed to the sentiments of its 17th C. progenitor.

Cromwell in the 19th C. had for many industrialists become an icon of the parliamentary system which they had learned to lobby in their own commercial interests. Not for nothing did the original painting of T.H. Maguire's popular engraving 'Cromwell Refusing the Crown of England' hang in the Bellevue home of Halifax's mill-owning Crossley family.

Four years after the Town Hall (as it was called at the time) was built, an American named George Henry Booth donated to Bradford a statue that was vastly superior to the local stone monarchs; namely a Carrara marble figure of Richard Cobden (1804–1865), M.P. for West Yorkshire. The statue was located in the Wool Exchange which has latterly succumbed to retail imperatives. Cobden now stands anomalously, a cobweb on his neck and with two joints of his little finger missing, in Waterstone's bookshop.

Cobden was a pacifist and tireless campaigner for free trade. He was particularly influential in persuading the Prime Minister, Robert Peel, to repeal the Corn Laws in 1846 (a period of history that bears interesting comparison to the Brexit crisis).

George Henry Booth had been a partner in 'Firth, Booth and Co' – a firm of stuff merchants that had been dissolved in 1872 ('stuff' was a generic term for woven fabrics).

It says much about the link between commercialism and parliament that Cobden's long-lived ally, the M.P. for Birmingham John Bright (1811–1889), was prevailed upon to unveil the statue. But most notable is an encomium by the *Bradford Observer* that compared Cobden to Cromwell, calling the latter "the incarnate genius of genuine Saxon liberty".

This view of Cromwell was largely promulgated by the historian Thomas Carlyle (who instigated the statue of Cromwell in Cambridge); the irony being that Cobden – who really should be better remembered – was unpersuaded[2] by Carlyle's hagiographic opinion of the Lord Protector...

Oliver Cromwell • Bradford

'Charles I' (1600–49); 'Oliver Cromwell' (1599–1658) and 'Charles II' (1630–85) by Farmer and Brindley Ltd., Lambeth

CONSTANTINE THE GREAT • YORK

There is no shortage of shrines and effigies in York, of course, but it is strangely deficient in statues. Maybe it's not York's thing. The city's best sculptor, G.W. Milburn (1844–1941), risked bankruptcy to give York its first public statue in 1885. Someone later knocked the nose off his version of Queen Victoria, and it was only when his statue of William Etty (1787-1849) outside the art gallery was recently restored that the local press[1] noticed that the artist's brush had been broken off *'at some point in the last 70 years'*.

No small credit, then, to York Civic Trust for commissioning the bronze statue of the Emperor Constantine from Philip Jackson in 1998. The justly celebrated Scot – whose safe pair of hands have spanned the gamut from Bobby Moore to Mahatma Gandhi – delivered a design that is both reposed and fabulously gestural.

Constantine was acclaimed as emperor by the army at 'Eboracum' (i.e. York) after his father's death in 306 AD. He is generally seen as the first Christian emperor, a position he only solidified after defeating his pagan challenger at the Battle of the Milvian Bridge in 312 AD. Jackson's sculpture supposedly captures Constantine contemplating the victory.

It still seems odd that the Trust didn't opt for Richard III, though. The 'son of York' puts in a comparatively rare appearance on the City

In the Capitoline Museum. Source Wikipedia

Hall in Bradford, although *(centre picture, above)* it's hardly a flattering design. The sculptor has gleefully taken up Shakespeare's propagandist lead, possibly echoing Harry Furniss's well-known sketch of Sir Henry Irving. A mis-shaped bag of curved bones, Richard clenches his right fist, the sword behind his legs symbolising thwarted ambition, while his brow furrows at the prospect of spending 500 years beneath the tarmac of a Leicester car park.

A still more interesting choice than Constantine might have been the Emperor Septimius Severus *(pictured above left)* who died in 'Eboracum' in 211. Severus

was the first black African-born Emperor of Rome; and there would have been a poetic quality had he become Yorkshire's first 'BAME' public statue

The low proportion of black figures among the UK's public statues surely warrants more attention. The supposed first examples – the 'Platform Pieces' made by Kevin Atherton for Brixton railway station – were almost incidental[2] and only date back to 1986. Sculptor Graham Ibbeson was involved in a campaign to erect a statue outside the grounds of Rotherham United to Arthur Wharton. But while there now is a statue to Wharton – 'Britain's first black footballer'

– it's outside St. George's Park in Staffordshire. You'd think there were enough contenders (David Oluwale, Champion Jack Dupree...Charlie Williams!) for Yorkshire to honour, but the best on offer appears to be Jaiprakash Shirgaoankar's bust of Mahatma Gandhi in Hull's Nelson Mandela Gardens. Tellingly, this was 'donated by Hull's Indian community' in 2018.

Meanwhile, in 2016 a homeless man named John Flanagan re-affirmed York's contempt for its statuary when he kicked the sword out from Constantine's hand and brandished it before sticking it in a drain. He was seen on CCTV and fined £783.

THE YOUNG WILBERFORCE • POCKLINGTON

The monstrous 102 foot monument in Wilberforce's birth-town of Hull and the effigy outside the Wilberforce Museum are sound but expectable statements. Sally Arnup's privately funded, 2007 bronze 'advertisement' for Pocklington School (which he attended from 1771 to 1776) is not.

Wilberforce[1] (1795–1833) was a Tory who bought his way into parliament and held that women had no place in public life. His role in the abolition of slavery has been overplayed at the expense of seminal figures such as Thomas Clarkson (1760–1846). He was short (5'4"), put a stone in his shoe to 'chafe his worldly pride' and was described by one contemporary as "an ugly, undignified man".

None of which preoccupied Arnup, quondam head of sculpture at York College of Art. While she used contemporary references for her 15-year old Wilberforce, the figure is highly idealised and has a lithe poise that you might expect from a nationally recognised animal sculptor.

'Voyage' • Sculpted by Steinunn Thorarinsdottir (b.1955)

VOYAGE • HULL

'Voyage' was a gift to Hull made by the town of Vik in Iceland in 2006. Steinunn Thorarinsdottir's trademark androgynous stylite is replicated by a similar figure in Vik harbour called 'For'. It's a richly meaningful work; if only because it records a centuries long relationship in which stranded Hull fishermen were given succour at Vik, thereby seeking to soften more recent memories of the decades-long 'Cod Wars' that ended in 1976.

"Of all the art projects I have been involved with, this has been by far the most special and meaningful," said Thorarinsdottir, an internationally recognised sculptor[1].

Fast forward to 2011 and – just before midnight on a Sunday night – a gang of blokes turn up and drag the 300kg statue from its basalt plinth and make off with it in a van.

As is typical of Hull, a £1,500 reward for its return was offered by private individuals, some of whom had lost family members at sea. It wasn't recovered and the council's insurance footed the £40,000 bill for its refabrication. The statue's scrap value was estimated at less than £1,800.

Hull's Lord Mayor Colin Inglis said: "They [the Icelanders] were amazed at the time that anybody would do it. I think that continues to be the case. They just can't believe that someone would stoop so low, really"[2].

'Dickie' Bird • Barnsley

Barnsley's College Square was notable for a loquacious young wanderer from Northamptonshire called Mike. He began one of those conversations that you have to *conclude* with an introduction ("... my name was Vic, by the way").

Mike was keen to offer a critique of a nearby flower bed, where the strongest coloured blooms were centred and the gentler hues were placed on the periphery. Mike felt that this was wrong.

My mouth must have liked Mike, for it suddenly expressed an apparently long-standing concern that the modern system of civic planting – which uses a continuous cycle of relocated nursery plants – makes a mockery of any garden's micro-ecology.

This spurred Mike on to relate how he had worked as a janitor for his uncle, a landlord in Chicago. Mike remarked that he had almost never seen 'old people' in Chicago; only young workers who burned themselves out to pay huge rents on small apartments that, to him, seemed no better than prisons.

I suggested that cities tended to become like civic flower beds; that a constant turnover of 'flowers in bloom' (metaphorically speaking) created an unstable ecology. Mike liked that. We shook hands ("...*my name was Vic, by the way*") and Mike moved

'Kitty' • Barnsley

on – carrying a bucket filled with a curious mix of electronics and gardening items.

This rewarding encounter took place near Graham Ibbeson's 2009 sculpture of the cricket umpire, Dickie Bird. It's a well-known piece that – like Ibbeson's famous 1999 statue of Eric Morecambe – benefits from its professional posture ('You're out!').

According to Brian Lewis[1] (who is compiling a book on Ibbeson) Bird was initially unaware of the offensive connotations of his raised finger. Presumably, then, he was surprised when the statue's bronze digit became repeatedly used as a perch for items of ladies' underwear which had become superfluous in the course of a night-out.

Bras and knickers gave way to condoms and even (on Halloween) a pumpkin, before the Council in 2013 decided that Dickie should be given a defensive, five foot tall plinth. The whole affair was treated with admirable aplomb; Dickie Bird (who had on occasion been witnessed removing the items) was unembarrassed, while Graham Ibbeson made an heroically honest remark to the *Daily Mail* for which he deserves unstinting reverence:–

"It's horrible when people abuse Dickie like that," Ibbeson said "But I must admit if I was a bit younger I would do the same thing myself"[2].

A few paces downhill from Dickie Bird is Ibbeson's memorial to the Oaks Colliery Disaster of 1866, in which a series of underground explosion claimed 361 lives. The 2017 sculpture cost £125,000, most of it raised by public contributions. Ibbeson (who had a distant relative that died in the explosion) gave his time for free.

Personally I struggle with Ibbeson's later, more photographic style (although I rather like the watch on Dickie Bird's left wrist; a vital umpiring tool!) and the Oaks memorial, no doubt for all the right reasons, strikes me as overworked. Its fictionalised figure ('Kitty') metamorphoses awkwardly between a lift-winding structure and a coal slide (which cascades behind her like the fins on Godzilla's back).

It seems less eloquent than the nearby veteran railway trucks whose brutal qualities feel more of a piece with history.

Barnsley's determination to celebrate itself betrays an anxiety that almost every post-industrial town has displayed since the Thatcher era. The nearby WW1 translucent memorials, the statues, the current banners of famous Barnsleyites – all variously lay eager claim to a past, present *and* a future. But you can't reasonably ask every instrument in an orchestra to sound the same note at the same time with the same volume; and it was a relief to move on next to Joseph Locke Park...

Joseph Locke • Barnsley

...So who was Joseph Locke? The fact that more-people-than-not will ask that question highlights the value of statues in the public realm. For while Locke – who stands shoulder to shoulder with his fellow engineers (and friends) Robert Stephenson and Isambard Kingdom Brunel – cannot possibly disappear from the halls of history, his candle evidently needs some kind of pilot light.

There's Locke Park itself, of course; donated to Barnsley by his widow, Phoebe, in 1862. And unlike the Sculpture Park further up the M1 whose roads are constipated with coaches; with people clinging onto the bull-bars of their Range Rovers as they change into over-engineered Alpine footwear; with saggy blokes in yellow vests and sunglasses squawking into their walkie-talkies, with people panting in pursuant dismay as their 'designer dogs' eke what joy they can from their crumbling, genetically deficient hips... unlike all of *that*, Locke Park on Sunday morning is peaceably packed with people walking their weekend relatives or watching their kids play (often in Polish), and with youngsters up to no good in the way that – frankly – they should be ("Let's climb on the statue"; "No, we'll do it later. Let that man take his photo").

A Canadian couple – drawn by the camera as much as his statue – come up and read about Joseph Locke. Born in Attercliffe, moved to Barnsley aged five: he went on to build half of Britain's railway network and more besides. A brilliant engineer, of course. George Stephenson declared the Woodhead Tunnel was impossible to build and that he'd eat the first steam train that went through it. It was Locke that served it up[1]. Mind you, the plaque probably didn't tell the Canadians that Locke was driving 'Rocket' when it killed William Huskisson M.P., the first ever railway casualty.

Around 70% of Barnsley's electorate voted for Brexit. So it seemed odd to discover that a ghostly clone of Locke's statue had been given to Barentin, the 'City of Arts' near Rouen which famously boasts hundreds of statues on its streets. You might assume (I did) that this was down to Carlo Marochetti.

The talented but reputedly toady Italian was Queen Victoria's favourite sculptor. He cast Landseer's lions in Trafalgar Square and his statue of Robert Stephenson outside Euston Station (installed in 1871) is an obvious companion piece to Joseph Locke (1866).

It turns out, however, that Locke built the striking viaduct at Barentin in 1846. It famously collapsed (albeit not Locke's fault) just before it was completed and had to be hastily rebuilt[2].

And so (recalling the conversation with 'Mike' alongside 'Dickie Bird') it comes forcibly to mind that sculpture parks, with their endlessly transplanted products, are a kind of 'civic roundabout' whose allure hides a blighted micro-ecology. Locke Park – where you are almost speared by a treecreeper as you sidestep an ice cream that is dying on the tarmac, before marvelling at the inept attempt of a sparrowhawk to hide in the tree canopy – feels happy. Feels healthy.

Photo: René & Peter van der Krogt, http://statues.vanderkrogt.net.

THE RUDSTON MONOLITH

Neolithic Standing Stone (c.2000 BCE) • All Saints Churchyard, Rudston, nr. Bridlington

The chief mystery of the Rudston Monolith is why it isn't better known. Perhaps, while it is the UK's tallest menhir at 7.6 metres tall, its width is slightly underwhelming. There's an argument that it is, in effect, taller yet. Not only has the top been broken off (the monument has been capped with lead at various points since the 18thC) but there is written evidence that the soil around the monolith was raised by over a metre when the churchyard was leveled in 1861.

The gritstone edifice could have come from Cayton, some 16km away but this – as much as the stone's original purpose – remains unclear. Supposedly the stone excited phallic rituals, while there's a claim (which can't be more than 150 years old) that it bears a dinosaur's footprint (experts are dubious!). It certainly has traces of historic, carved graffiti at its base. In a way it's surprising that there isn't more of this (Byron didn't hesitate to scratch his monika on the temple at Sounion, for instance) but presumably the site's sacred reputation discouraged taggers through the ages.

The formal picture *(left)* suggests that the Neolithic monument dominates its environs while the truth is that it has been jealously ambushed by Christian iconography *(far right)*. The dominant local fable has it the other way around, of course: it's because the pagan site was 'defiled' by the original (but long gone) Norman church that the Devil hurled the stone at it. He missed. Again[1].

THE OTLEY BULL STONE

Neolithic Standing Stone (C.2000 BCE) • Otley Chevin

By contrast with the Rudston Monolith, the six-foot high Bull Stone is unimpeded by any nearby objects beyond the odd low-flying aircraft from Yeadon Airport. Indeed the stone barely seems to be publicly accessible and you wonder if the collapsed wall nearby hasn't been caused by latter-day, would-be druids stumbling drunkenly towards it prior to some solstice dawn.

On my visit a sheep skull had been placed next to the obelisk, but more intriguing was the anomalous chunk of stone at its base (which isn't shown on the 1956 sketch featured on Paul Bennett's excellent 'Northern Antiquarian' website[1], so it's probably nothing to get excited about).

The mystery of the Bull Stone (which wasn't archaeologically recorded before 1880) lies in its name.

The most cited origin is that bulls were tethered to it before being baited by dogs; followed by references to a 'bull-steann' (old Yorkshire dialect for a whetstone). Bennett speculates that, 'Boul' being a defunct term of contempt for an old man, it could relate to the devil – but points out that the name 'Boul Stones' is recorded from the mid-19th C. onwards, whereas earlier references talk of the 'Boon Stones'. 'Boons' is yet another old word for 'reapers' and Bennet cites a widespread superstition that such stones were once harvesters who worked too late and were turned to stone by various night time spirits...

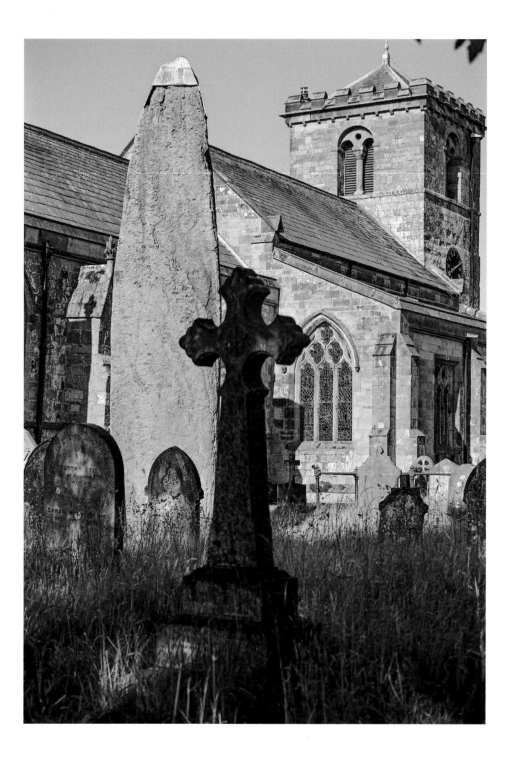

'TRAIN' • DARLINGTON

David Mach's 1997 'Train' is easy to see but hard to find. Once sighted from the A66 you are deflected into a Minotaur's delight of industrial units that surround a Morrisons Superstore. Only the truly committed will find an apologetic car park and an idyllic walk through bog asphodels and bulrushes that up-tips them before this superlative monument to Darlington's railway history.

In a sense, 'Train' doesn't belong in this book. Darlington is on the wrong side of the North Yorks. border. But the LNER Class A4 was actually built in Doncaster; while the architects, structural engineers and surveyors involved in getting the 181,754 bricks in the right order all came from Leeds and Bradford – and the firm that actually built it was headquartered in York.

Gateshead's 'Angel of the North' was unveiled less than a year later than 'Train'. Both were controversial. The *Northern Echo*[1] website has a memorable picture of dour politicians brandishing leaflets declaiming 'Stop Labour's Train'. It cost too much, it looked ugly, it wasn't wanted...

Much the same was said about Antony Gormley's monument (which cost at least £100,000 more) but while the 'Angel...' has accreted a regional sense of pride, Mach's 'Train' is slowly being forgotten. Why? The work succeeds as a spectacle, it invokes communal history and it achieves a happy synthesis with Mach's body of work.

It might well be in a less-than-ideal location but no less is the 'Angel...', while people happily trekked out to see Sean Henry's 'Seated Man' during its tenure on far-flung Castleton Rigg[2].

The ease with which 'Train's' protective fence is circumvented gives the game away.

A half-hearted nod to Health & Safety, it merely spoils any tourist photographs. There is no 'ownership' here. Rather than uniting a community, 'Train' has come to embody its divisions.

"...In years to come, people will come to see 'Train' in the same way they go to Trafalgar Square or the Pyramids," claimed David Mach in 1997.

And it might happen yet, but only if the town can stop chewing its liver out, or – more likely – if someone makes a movie about vampires taking up residence in 'Train's' discreetly incorporated bat boxes...

THE BRICK MAN • LEEDS

It has become *de rigeur* to mock the Leeds Councillors who refused planning permission for 'The Brick Man' in 1988.

Then comparatively unknown, Antony Gormley had entered and won a competition in 1986 to site a sculpture on the Holbeck triangle near Leeds railway station. His proposal was for a 30m high, hollow figure that people would be able to access via the heel and which would have had 'viewing windows' in the ears.

The vote to deny planning permission was reputedly a marginal one, influenced by partisan politics and with misgivings being expressed about the crotch area of the sculpture.

Such small-mindedness meant that Leeds missed out on an icon that the *Guardian* could have used instead of Gormley's 'Angel of the North' whenever it needed to pretend it was still a northern paper.

What is less often remarked is that a *Yorkshire Evening Post* phone poll at the time found that most of its readers didn't want the Brick Man either. Nor need this have been mere philistinism. Gormley's stock in the arts community – which is substantially unimpressed with his endless 'collective body' sculptures – is not that high.

The experience of David Mach's 'Train' in Darlington suggests that the Brick Man's proposed cost of £600,000 would soon have risen; while there's a case to be made that the public find brick to be insufficiently 'artistic' for them to take it to heart as a 'serious monument'.

Which isn't to say that an opportunity wasn't missed; just to emphasise that opportunities are by definition ambiguous. Had it been built, the Brick Man could well have 'failed to thrive'.

So while it might be a Pyrrhic victory, it's interesting to reflect how the permanent presence (and popularity) of Gormley's maquette in Leeds City Art Gallery has swelled in significance as a cautionary reminder about making timid decisions when considering imaginative schemes[1].

ERNIE WISE • MORLEY

The fact that John Eric Bartholomew changed his name to Eric Morecambe, but Ernest Wiseman didn't become Ernie Morley suggests at least one flaw in the thinking behind the Ernie Wise sculpture in his 'home town'.

The success of Graham Ibbeson's 1999 'dancing Eric' sculpture in Morecambe no doubt spiced the appetite for a counterpart monument – but overlooked the harsh truth that when it comes to comedy duos nobody loves the straight man.

The statue's committee might have taken the hint when its 2008 request for £38,000 of National Lottery money for a bronze statue of 'little Ern' was turned down. Undeterred –– and encouraged by an £8,000 pledge from Doreen Wiseman, Ernie's widow – they plumped instead for a stone statue budgeted at £10,000.

The result, unveiled in 2010, is truthfully not much loved. "It doesn't even look like him. It looks as if he's falling over and it's frightening people," one resident told the BBC[1].

Like one of Michelangelo's 'Captives' Ernie emerges from an effluent pile of stone, holding an umbrella that would put most truncheons to shame. What appears to be an avalanche of scrambled egg pours down his neck from inside a hat that is thicker than a toilet seat.

The choice of Dewsbury sculptor, Melanie Wilks, becomes understandable when you discover the happier statues she provided a few years earlier outside Morley's Town Hall. Ernie's face is recognisable if you look *down* on the figure *(picture right)* but verisimilitude is not really Wilks' strength.

Meanwhile someone recently tried to saw the leg off Graham Ibbeson's Eric Morecambe statue. Is there any consolation to be had in the knowledge that – because they tend to be melted down for armaments - bronze statues traditionally survive history less well than stone ones? Perhaps not.

ERNIE WISE
1925~1999

THE BLACK PRINCE • LEEDS

There is a wonderful 1954 picture of the Black Prince in his original setting by Magnum photographer Marc Riboud that conveys the significance that public statues had before advertising and architectural statements came to dominate street furniture. The image somehow means more than the oft-repeated facts, which are that...

The statue was commissioned by Colonel Thomas Walter Harding, a pin factory magnate and Lord Mayor of Leeds (1898–99). The intention was to enhance Leeds' city status that had been granted in 1893 and – in the absence of a sufficiently grand regional figure – the Black Prince was chosen from a shortlist of 'unused' options that included the Prince's father, Edward III; Henry V, and the Duke of Marlborough. The sculptor Thomas Brock (but lately celebrated for his statue of Prince Albert in the eponymous memorial) was selected. He spent seven years devising the piece, which had to be cast in Belgium as there were no English foundries large enough. It was unveiled in 1903.

The Prince was surrounded by a balustrade on which were perched allegorical figures of Morn and Eve made by Alfred Drury (1856-1944). Drury made similar gatepost figures for Brock's later Victoria Memorial in London's Mall. Drury's figures were always mildly controversial but only for their nudity. It seems pertinent now, though, to question why the female figures in City Square were allowed to be generic but the male figures had to be specific. Of the four 'wise men' near the post office Dr Walter Hook and Frank Harrison are Leeds figures but comparatively undistinguished; James Watt is distinguished but has no more connection with Leeds than the Black Prince. Only Joseph Priestley (another Drury figure) meets both requirements.

Imposing, slightly tasteless and desperate for authenticity... is what it all boils down to. The square was re-modelled in 2003 but not enough to hold at bay the commercial adaptation of the old post office. The opportunistic inclusion of local boy Ken Armitage's otherwise delightful 'Legs Walking' italicises the impression that the City Square serves as a kind of civic lumber room. But hey... at least it's busy.

John Metcalfe • Knaresborough

We live, so our betters assure us, in egalitarian times and the life-sized, intimate statue that invites fraternisation is increasingly encountered in public sites. This can easily lead to a false 'right-on' quality (especially when the figures are representative of lost or disappearing trades) but you would be hard put to think of a better commoner to ennoble in bronze than John Metcalfe (aka 'Blind Jack of Knaresborough') who had an extraordinary life.

Born to an impoverished family and blind from the age of six (due to smallpox), Metcalfe played the violin and oboe, fought at the battle of Culloden and – his main claim to fame – surveyed and oversaw the construction of 180 miles of road across Yorkshire, Lancashire and Derbyshire.

A campaign by 'local entrepreneur' Terry Maude raised £30,000 and led to local sculptor Barbara Asquith being commissioned to make Knaresborough's statue of Metcalfe, which was unveiled in 2009.

And suitably flushed with success, Maude then set about raising £43,000 to commission another Harrogate sculptor, Chris Kelly, to create a comparable effigy in 2017 of Knaresborough's other great icon, Old Mother Shipton.

The two works don't exactly 'gel'. Old Ma Shipton is finely detailed, buried in witchy artefacts and surrounded by a verbose pavement script. Blind Jack is more comfortably gestural, hugging his surveyor's wheel and staring into the distance of his imagination.

You're invited to sit next to either figure on weight-bearing benches that are themselves works of art; but you rarely see people eating their chips next to the witchy one.

Knaresborough has a distinct crust of retired affluence these days and it's tempting to make snide comparisons with towns such as Market Weighton who couldn't afford one bronze statue, let alone two.

The irony, of course, is that you'd be hard put to think of anywhere else in the country that has two statues which are not only commoners but where one of them is an old woman and the other is a disabled man.

Need it be added that both statues attract tourists like a newly-washed car attracts bird lime?

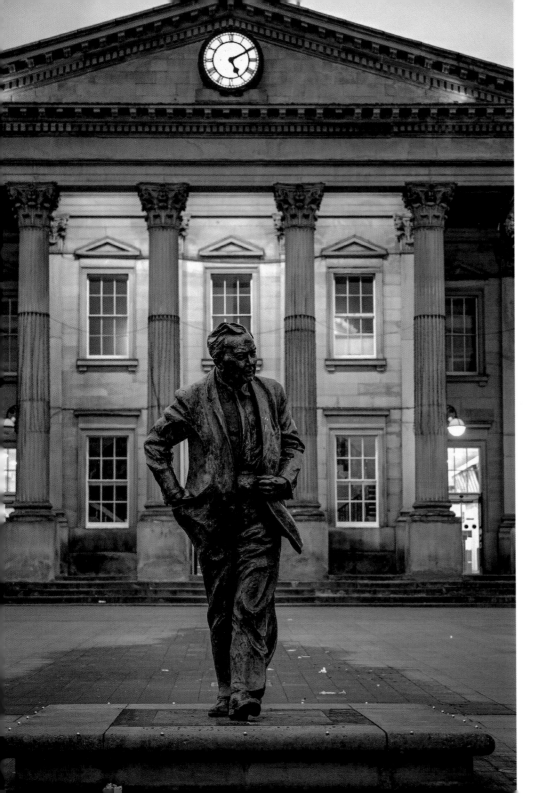

HAROLD WILSON • HUDDERSFIELD

I arrived at dawn (5.10am) on a Saturday morning in the hope that carousing Huddersfieldians would have put a traffic cone on Harold Wilson's head. Alas, despite the presence of a pair of stacked cones, an empty bottle under a bench and a trio of remnant party-goers he was unadorned.

Wilson, a major figure out of tune with the present, feels at home in a town that was struggling even before the economy eloped with the financial markets. Wilson, like Rugby League, was of course born in Huddersfield – although the George Hotel where the latter happened is boarded up; its Union Jack contorted and frayed in a meta-phor for the destructive process of Brexit. The contrast with Barnsley's brash bravura could not be more marked.

The sculptor Ian Walters was a committed socialist who entered the competition to make Wilson's statue at the behest of Tony Benn M.P.. It was unveiled by Labour Prime Minister Tony Blair in 1999.

Walters based Wilson's stance on a series of photographs from the 1964 election – and from one angle the tilted shoe, the twisted head and the akimbo arm seem perfect. From another angle the phleg-my-voiced Prime Minister seems macroce-phalic and plain gimbly.

Mary Wilson famously insisted that her husband should not be depicted with his trademark pipe as this might trivialise him. She later suggested it is actually what he was reaching for in his right-hand pocket[1].

Fred Trueman • Skipton

There was a feeling in 2010 that the £90,000 sculpture of fast bowler Fred Trueman should have been sited at Headingley cricket ground and not in Skipton's canal basin.

But even though his installation ousted a maple tree, the erstwhile Dales resident is pretty well accepted nowadays.

There's a rumour that (as with Harold Wilson) the sculptor had to cope with family injunctions about "Fiery Fred's" appearance; yet the statue shows him happily at work, which is all you could reasonably ask.

Unless, of course, it was actually *insisted* that he had Sonic the Hedgehog's hair…

WOMEN OF STEEL • SHEFFIELD

Sheffield Council should be acknowledged for the management of its public sculptures, which occur throughout the city with a placement worthy of a chess grandmaster.

To take but two examples, Richard Perry's contemporary memorial to Thomas Boulsover (1705-88) cutely invokes the concave/convex feature of the Sheffield Plate Process that he invented *(pictured below)*; while it's admirable that 'the Christian Poet', James Montgomery[1] (1771-1854) was rescued from dilapidation in the 1970s at a time when contemporary

prejudice would tend to see him consigned to forgotten 'realms of glory' *(pictured below centre)*.

Sheffield created something of an icon in 2016 with Martin Jennings' 'Women of Steel' – a tribute in Barkers Pool to the women who worked in the city's armaments factories during the war.

The campaign for the monument's erection was led by surviving WW2 workers and raised £170,000 . The statue was launched with a pop song, although its seems more in tune with Gracie Fields' 'Sing as We Go'.

Public sensibilities tend to be dictated by propaganda and there is more than a whiff of Stakhanovism about the pair that isn't (for instance) found in Ray Lonsdale's steel workers tribute in Scunthorpe; while George Fullard's nearby 'Angry Woman' sculpture somehow evokes a more

pertinent civilian horror at being bombed. As Alma Bottomley told the *Sheffield Star* about her experience of making tank tracks during World War 2 : "To be honest, it wasn't very pleasant[2]".

In many ways the garlands heaped on Jennings' sculpture had more to do with the

debate about the lack of women in public statuary. It has been estimated that only 15% of public statues depict women.

Sad to relate that the long-mooted plans to raise a £4.2m contender to the 'Angel of the North' near Rotherham[3] is dubbed the 'Steel MAN'... one step forward, eh?

Ray Lonsdale illustrates nothing so much as the gulf between the art world and the caravan-owning public.

Nobody who ever cherished a dream could be anything but glad for his success; but the work is as subtle as a publican's greeting. It is popular though. In 2014 the residents

of Seaham, Co. Durham raised £60,000 to keep Lonsdale's huge sculpture of a WW1 soldier ('1101' or 'Tommy' as it's now dubbed) on its seafront... thereby shaming the Council into paying the remaining £85,000. In 2011 Scarborough residents had started a similar campaign for 'Freddie Gilroy and the Belsen

Stragglers', only to be pre-empted by a pensioner ("She's not a rich lady, she has been a saver her entire life"[1]) who paid out £55,000 on their behalf.

Lonsdale had 'loaned' both works to the towns in the first instance, which was certainly a fiscal risk, but also a canny one.

The 'Scunthorpe Steelworkers Sculpture' was slightly different. A team led by an ex-mayor spent seven years raising the requisite £48,000 from various companies to 'celebrate 125 years of steel making', Notably, a portion of the cash was stumped up by the Arts Council of England (ACE).

The fact that ACE is committed to 'excellence in the arts' was presumably no small consolation to Lonsdale, who spent years as a maintenance fitter in Sunderland and gave up a trial arts degree ("...it wasn't for me") before taking the plunge and risking his bin-making company by switching his output to sculpture.

Lonsdale is unashamedly interested in the story behind his figures, but Fred Gilroy (1921–2008) seems to have been immortalised simply because the sculptor had befriended him. He was one of the soldiers who liberated the Belsen concentration camp in April 1945 but has no particular relevance to Scarborough and the term 'stragglers' is not indicative of a particular anecdote. He was an ordinary bloke who

witnessed an appalling passage of history. That's as profound as it gets.

Again, the Scunthorpe sculpture is slightly different. The figures are generic and the scene is taken from the 1940s – a period which enables Lonsdale to depict a woman worker. They also lack "Gilroy's" scale – which is a blatant part of Lonsdale's appeal. His chosen material (Cor-ten steel) is ironically a patented *American* alloy whose rusted patina serves to protect its integrity (it's the stuff that the 'Angel of the North' is made of).

In May 2019 a determined 'scrote' decided to climb on top of the Scunthorpe sculpture and the photo of him stood on its head aroused instant wrath ("No respect at all, it's a disgrace"[2]). On the eve of Holocaust Memorial Day someone threw yellow paint onto Freddie Gilroy's lap, leading to comparable outrage ("mindless and pathetic act"[3]).

It's no good complaining that his work looks like those unconvincing 3D wooden 'slot kit' dinosaurs that aunties buy dismayed kids, or being snide about the Pinterest site that offers the "80 best Ray Lonsdale sculptures". The public has voted and the media is persuaded. Best, perhaps, to acknowledge the regard of his fans, the inescapable draw of his scale and the occasional detail which – however awkwardly manifested – poses a valid question to more groomed talents. There are not, for example, too many sculptures with fags in their mouths.

Walking Man • Sheffield

George Fullard is 'the real thing'. A proper artist. Or so it struck me when I first saw his work at a show in the Mappin in 1998. But does that make him a suitable public sculptor?

A miner's son from Darnall, Fullard studied art at Sheffield College, went to the RCA and subsequently plunged into a notable academic career that spawned at least two major, contemporary 'names' (Phyllida Barlow and David Nash).

He also had a tough war. He witnessed the bombing of Sheffield in 1940 and was seriously injured at the battle of Cassino. And the work shows it. But here's the thing. This is an extract from a book[1] that describes Fullard's 'Walking Man' statue that is now (after multiple re-sitings) striding in front of Sheffield's Winter Gardens.

"Fullard's 'Walking Man' (1957)... seems tantalisingly to gesture from the object tradition toward the more active, experiential trend through its represented activity: walking. The focus is beginning to shift away

from the objects themselves and towards the spaces between them, the viewer's experience of negotiating that space, and the embodied experience of the encounter."

I think we can agree that *that* is bollocks. Here though is Fullard himself:–

"The need of art is that the artist attains absolute conviction of the inevitable occurrence of miracles through the power of instinct and imagination. Just as the child without effort, slips through imagination out of life to make a man out of a pepper pot, or the heaving deck of a shipwreck of a placid pavement, so the artist works towards the miracle of making visible that which apparently could not exist... The easy magic of the child is an element of

life. To find the parallel in art demands the total attendance of consciousness. And at the heart of the innocent, the new infancy for which the artist works, lies the core of humility not as a public process or a technique, but as a profound secret".[2]

It's no easier to read than the first text, I grant, but it's got content and heart. Seek Fullard out, particularly the assemblages... because he seems to me to be stranded between two cultures and the sculptures don't necessarily 'work' in the public realm.

There are three Fullard figures in the Congregational Chapel gardens on Norfolk

Street, each of which have an intrigue and strength that out-punches most public sculpture; yet they clearly don't agree with the space, nor with each other. The irony is that most of the figures were posthumously cast from a 1957 exhibition called 'Looking at People'.

Only the 'Walking Man' has truthfully tightroped its way out of an art space into acceptance by the public. The proof of it was apparent during his tenure at the Town Hall. While there "he was often variously seen with a cigarette stuck between his lips, a beer tucked can under his arm, or a traffic cone placed on his head..."[3]. Now you can't do better than that.

rhs.org.uk/chatsworth

Your visit supports our work as a charity

RHS Registered Charity no. 222879 / SC038262

Partnered by

WEDGWOOD
ENGLAND 1759

sandwich deli &
fair trade coffee bar

WALKING MAN
1957 BRONZE BY
GEORGE FULLARD

The Lovers • Doncaster

Public sculptures don't just fade away; someone decides to *take* them away. A monument's obscurity may be tolerated, but only if it's not actively impeding other plans. Political opinion can, of course, prove fatal – as witness the lot of numberless Lenins and Stalins that followed the break-up of the Soviet Union, or the neglected Raj statues mustered in New Delhi's Coronation Park.

It remains to be seen whether the freshly perceived misogyny and racism inherent in the statues of past eras will be tolerated by the new 'liberal' era. On the one hand there is the ongoing controversy over memorialized Confederate figures in the Southern States of America. On the other hand there is the unexpected restitution of Moscow's 'Park of Fallen Monuments' into a kind of Soviet Disneyland[1], or the recent decision to actually *restore* Coronation Park.

"We preserve Mughal-era monuments so it is only natural that we should seek to preserve the history of the British period," the Indian historian leading the latter project was recently quoted in the *Daily Telegraph*[2]. "We are not living in the past but learning from it".

Could it be, then, that 'fashion' is a greater danger to sculpture than politics? Fifteen years ago the 'Drury Girls' in Leeds were very nearly 'retired' as *passé* objects of Victorian fancy. There are photographs from one of Yorkshire's larger conurba-

tions that show fragments of a modernist statue in a skip that we can't print because it would lose the photographer his job (he's a council worker who enacted the deed at his employer's behest).

Nobody wants to spend resources on the maintenance and restoration of unfashionable items; and while bronze generally persists out-of-mind, many other materials do not. Which makes the restoration of 'The Lovers' – a painted GRP statue – a quietly extraordinary event. Erected in Doncaster's Arndale Centre (now the Frenchgate Centre) in 1967, 'The Lovers' is an improbable piece of ecstatic eroticism that routinely attracted words like 'saucy', 'risqué' and, of course, 'outrage'.

Not unlike Paul Day's savagely deprecated statue, 'The Meeting Place', in Euston Station ("...a very good example of the crap out there," said Antony Gormley) – 'The Lovers' is said to have been a regular rendezvous point for (in this case) the hot-pant and maxi-skirt generation. It was eventually removed in the 1980s and put 'into storage' (a euphemism which seems to have involved someone's garden and then a car park).

It re-appeared in 2015 after the new owners of Doncaster's (rather strange) Waterside Shopping Centre realised that they had inherited the piece and decided to capitalise on any associated memories it might retain by restoring it.

Richard Bannister, from St. Modwen Properties described 'The Lovers' as "an icon for Doncaster" and it *is* somehow more endearing than the 2012 Danum Sculpture in Sir Nigel Gresley Square (even if the latter did cost £60,000).

Meanwhile, St. Modwen Properties got a further frisson of publicity when the statue's origination came to light following a chance conversation in Australia between a Doncaster woman and the wife of Australian architect Eckehart Selke.

Selke was a student on work placement in the UK between 1964 and 1967 and had been invited to visit the inchoate mall and devise a possible centrepiece for it. On his return he presented a pencil sketch to his architect boss, who felt it was 'totally inappropriate' but who agreed to show it to the owners anyway.

Selke returned to Australia shortly afterwards and only realised that the sketch had been reified when he stumbled on a picture on the internet in the late 1980s – by which time it was 'in storage'. Selke and his wife made a special visit to see the restored work in 2016.

Sadly, the over-enthusiastic frotage of the Doncaster climate is now causing 'The Lovers' to flake anew. As George Harrison noted in the 1970s, 'all things must pass' – but it's interesting to ponder precisely what it is here that Doncaster stands to lose.

PHILIP LARKIN • HULL

The fact that sculptor Martin Jennings studied English literature at Oxford (he also fashioned the Betjeman statue at St. Pancras) is possibly the only thing that Philip Larkin would have approved about his seven-foot high statue on Hull Paragon Interchange.

The statue, which was dressed in amber and black for the 2014 F.A. Cup, is constantly harried by the *hoi-polloi*. Shortly after it was unveiled in 2010 Larkin's spectacles were even bent out of shape by what the *Hull Daily Mail* unabashedly called "a drunken moron".

The statue stands on a surfboard whose text testifies to its inspiration by Larkin's poem *'The Whitsun Weddings'* (... lest anyone thought it was the *'High Windows'* behind him... arf!). Other excerpts from Larkin's slim collected works were later blobbed around the concourse but not, of course, the eight-word phrase about parenthood for which he is best remembered.

Larkin initially hated Hull. "What a hole, what witless, crapulous people," he wrote. But he ultimately warmed to its charms: "Oh yes, well, it's very nice and flat for cycling".

ANDREW MARVELL • HULL

Even though he was an incomparably greater poet than Larkin, I had intended (so far as this book was concerned) to leave Milton's pal Andrew Marvell 'standing and waiting'… but the happy simultaneity of "Jim the pot-man" *(right)* was too much to resist.

"Why…?" I asked Jim; and (despite the rain) received an account of his garb that involved a history of the 15th C. Hanseatic Wars and the origin of the word 'factory'. I'll spare you that.

William Day Keyworth Junior is notable for carving the (now substantially melted) lions outside Leeds Town Hall and for committing suicide *before* he made an equestrian statue

(q.v. Thorneycroft, Scheemakers, et al.). His marble statue of Andrew Marvell is handsome enough but perhaps what is truly notable about it is that it has been moved four times since it was presented to the City by Councillor John Winship in 1867.

It's been moved from the Town Hall to one end of George Street in 1902, then the other end of George Street in 1922, then to William Gee School in 1963 and latterly to its present and happy position in 1999.

Maybe Hull doesn't like metaphysical poets. Or maybe they want to keep Andy confused so that he doesn't return to the small village of Winestead which was his actual birthplace.

Amy Johnson(s) • Hull

The signs on Hawthorne Avenue were not good. Specifically, they were anacoluthons. "Welcome to Amy Johnson – an exciting range of 2 & 3 bedroom homes".

Eh what...?

The truth of Amy Johnson's life presumably lies somewhere between the circus antics that gave birth to that perennially infectious, close-rhymed ditty (*"Amy, wonderful Amy, how can you blame me for loving you"*) and the solid and (for the pilots) squalid heroics of early aviation.

Stephen Melton's 2016 bronze statue of Johnson (*picture right*) marked the 75th anniversary of her death. It is sited close to her childhood home and there is a duplicate statue near the scene of her tragic demise at Herne Bay. There's every reason for the effigy to feel authentic.

Unfortunately the earnest, gender challenging texts scribed onto her figure blend awkwardly with the Estate Agent gloss of 'Amy Johnson Square'. Novelist Vladimir Nabokov would have called it 'poshlost': the right message, but the wrong Amy.

The 1973 Portland Stone statue of Johnson on Prospect Street cost £3,000 and was funded by public subscription. Harry Ibbetson's figure stands modestly beside a washing machine-sized podium, looking a little dumpy in what might be an adapted welding suit. Ironically the contrast with the podium's text creates an affecting solemnity.

"Amy Johnson C.B.E. 1903–41. Pioneer Airwoman. Born 1st July at 154 St George's Rd Hull. She made record flights from England to Australia in 1930 (solo, 19 days) and to India (solo, 6 days). In 1931, to Japan (11 days) and Cape Town (solo, 4 days). In 1933, to U.S.A.. In 1934, to India. In 1936, to Cape Town and back. She died on active service January 5th 1941. May her fame live on."

That should surely be enough to inspire 'little princesses' to 'manly acts'. Melton's contemporary 'take' of a thigh-slapping panto gal in camera-pleasing leatherware seems at the very least a mixed message.

Meantime, try this. Put your top teeth on your bottom lip and try to smile without moronically wrinkling your nose.

No. I couldn't do it, either.

"WE WOMEN ARE JUST NOW ON THE THRESHOLD OF A CAREER WHICH HAS SO FAR BEEN REGARDED AS THE STRICT PROVINCE OF MAN — THAT OF AERONAUTICAL ENGINEERING"

MARCH 1932

Amy Johnson Square

Delivered by Keepmoat Homes
in partnership with
Hull City Council 2018

Keepmoat Homes   Hull City Council

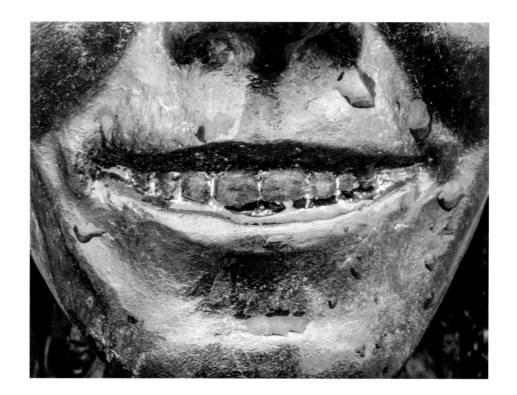

Diving Belle
Scarborough

Perhaps the most surprising claim about the 'Diving Belle' is that it was the first statue to be erected since Scarborough gained its obligatory Queen Victoria; which would make the Belle's companion piece ('The Bathing Belle') the town's third statue.

The Georgian era 'Bathing Belle' represents the seaside resort's 'past' (an 18th C. gentlewoman, metaphorically drowning in demure cambric); while the 'Diving Belle' (a liberated car mascot fearlessly displaying her galvanised steel cellulite) is the 'future'.

Both works were commissioned at £40,000 a piece by the Civic Society from a Sunderland blacksmith called Craig Knowles. His Facebook page boasts how his commercial skillset ranges from "interior furniture, gates and railings to large public sculptures".

It's not the most promising advertisement and Scarborough arguably got lucky.

The 'Bathing Belle' lacks the modest but effective illusion of disequilibrium displayed by her companion on Vincent Pier and has been 'retired' from view at least once.

'Diving Belle' (2007) • Sculpted by Craig Knowles

The four-metre high fisherman on Filey's Coble Landing is another of Ray Lonsdale's outsized, Cor-ten steel whimsies that was bought for the East Coast by Maureen Robinson – a pensioner who (up to 2018) contributed a regular 'walks column' to the *Scarborough News*.

The statue had worked its way down from Saltburn to Whitby to Filey before getting caught in Maureen's philanthropic net[1]. Now adopted as a tribute to Filey's fishing history, you can't help but wonder if a memorial to the Butlins Holiday Camp, which closed in 1984 and brought the town most of its popular renown, might have been more appropriate.

As ever, Lonsdale has graced the work with a poem (indiscriminately described as a 'powerful statement' on the internet[2]) and with the characteristically quirky addition of a pilfering rat at his feet (prompting the thought that there are not too many sculptures outside of Hamlein that feature rats).

As with 'Freddie Gilroy' in Scarborough, the Sunderland sculptor's work is an absolute camera magnet. It's a perfect companion to the giant lobster on the abutting 'crazy golf' course, and in 2017 was enshrined on the packet of "a new flavour of Yorkshire Crisps, a mix of oyster, chilli and lemon"[3].

WILLIAM BRADLEY • MARKET WEIGHTON

I loved Market Weighton. Its passing denizens were terrifyingly friendly and the town's hyperbolic sense of its history[1] was utterly of-a-piece with having fostered William Bradley, England's tallest man.

Ironically "The Yorkshire Giant's" faithfully represented height of 7'9" is diminished by the sculptural convention of magnifying a subject's actual size by at least 25%. Ray Lonsdale's fisherman at Filey stands an unwarranted four-feet higher than Bradley, while – at seven feet high – even Hull's pedestrian Philip Larkin comes up to his shoulders.

A disarmingly honest plaque explains the genesis of the Bradley sculpture which it was originally hoped would be bronze. The extended time required to raise the monies for this led "...Stuart Barbor of Woodlands Nurseries to formulate an idea" the plaque informs us. Walking his own woodland, Barbor found an aging oak that had probably been growing when Bradley was performing his various feats 200 years ago.

"Geoff Hall of Market Weighton Area Businesses Ltd" was shown the tree and it was duly felled and delivered by "'Jibbo' and 'Banksy' (Martin Jibson and Geoff Banks)" towards the end of 2006 so that "Malcolm MacLachlan – a wood sculptor of Tibthorpe" could work on it over the winter period.

A cynic might suggest that the result is not a lot different from a 'Cigar Store Indian[2]', while the durability of the wooden statue – which had to be spruced up in 2018 – clearly won't compare to bronze. Thenagain (putting aside museum pieces) 'Big Bill' is easily the most notable wooden statue in Yorkshire and commands an instant charm, not least because he is so completely indigenous.

The ONLY distressing features are the padlocks. It's almost a primeval impulse to want to stroke a polished piece of wood. Isn't it? William is stood on a leveled platform, graced with steps and a wheelchair access ramp... but ringed with a locked palisade.

THE GANSEY GIRL • BRIDLINGTON

The East Riding of Yorkshire Council and Bridlington Harbour Commission funded 'The Gansey Girl' on Bridlington's harbour wall as part of the Maritime Trail. It is primarily intended as a tourist attraction.

While it might weather down, the sandstone block on which the figure sits seems anomalous and the little fishes pinned to it (bearing the names of harbour families) seem misplaced.

The figure itself is nicely judged, though, and its quality of authenticity is explained when artist Stephen Carvill (in an excellent YouTube video[1]) reveals it was inspired by a late 19th C. photograph[2] taken by Whitby's Frank Meadow Sutcliffe (1853-1941).

'Ganseys' (derived from 'Guernseys') were knitted, one-piece jumpers. Legend has it that the bodies of drowned fishermen were often identified by the different knitting styles of East Coast towns and – intended or not – there's a distinct melancholy about the piece.

The 'Gansey Girl' has evidently been a local success, celebrated by the local press[3] and even made available on a tee-shirt[4].

To a modest degree it has also succeeded in embodying the town's identity; with the consequence that (as of Summer 2019) Bridlington is being urged by 'regeneration chiefs' to get itself in a froth over plans for another sculpture by "an international artist" whose subject matter is still under wraps[5].

When 'Gansey Girl' was installed an excited 'regeneration chief' let slip plans for a sculpture which would commemorate the little-known fact that Bridlington was the first town in England to witness surfing. The event occurred in September 1890 during the visit of two Hawaiian princes.

If the sculpted royal surfers were ever installed, I never found them... but the present game of suspense highlights the curiously haphazard process by which sculptures are selected.

Steve Carvill – a local artist whose profile has surely been boosted by 'Gansey Girl' – is promoting his own table-top, limited edition bronze of T.E.Lawrence[6], who was stationed (happily, so it is said) at RAF Bridlington shortly before his death. It's based on a photograph of Lawrence on a bike leaning against a wall in the town. It's almost designed to be a modern, informal sculpture... but would that alone justify its enlarged, public installation?

THE DOTTEREL SHEPHERD AND SHEEP • REIGHTON

The shepherd with his dog and five sheep on the A165 near the Dotterel pub was intended to be a 'feelgood piece' which recalled the area's rural history. The sculptor, Ronald Falck, also made 'The Anchorman' (2015) on Bridlington Harbour,

Both pieces have an air of caricature which might be put down to Falck's technique of physically sculpting GRP matting on iron frames (as distinct from using moulds). At any rate, caricature should not be mistaken for naivety. Falck was formally trained; had graduated from the Slade Schools in 1960, and could claim to have been taught by such 'high art' luminaries as William Coldstream, Henry Moore and Ernst Gombrich.

Falck's late forays into sculpture (he died in 2018) evidently met with no small resistance from local councilors. Despite offering to pay for all or much of the work that he proposed around Bridlington his suggestions were repeatedly rebuffed – or so (writing in 2015) he claims on his still extant website[1].

Falck here details his frustrations at duplicitous committees and bewails the absence of good public sculpture in Bridlington. He would almost certainly have berated this book for its inaccuracies (not least the slipshod tendency to use the word 'sculpture' and 'statue' as if they were near synonyms). Falck concludes his misgivings about Bridlington's authorities in hieratic mode:–

"It is in his faith being an artist – which is a kind of religion to him, and because art is spiritual, that his values within his creativity are among the eternal contribution to humanity, but people do not always realise that a developed perception is needed to make value judgments about art. Time is needed to evaluate the worth of art products, not money. What must we change to help us achieve those ideal values which speak of our time in this modern world?"

James Cook RN • Whitby

The Captain Cook statue in Whitby should not, of course, be confused with Captain Cook's Monument at Roseberry Topping… and technically neither of them should be deemed pertinent to 'Captain Cook' (since he never actually held the rank, but leapfrogged from commander in 1775 to the superior rank of post-captain).

Presented to the town of Whitby by the Hon Sir Gervase Becket, M.P. on 2nd October 1912, the 7'6" bronze statue is the work of John Tweed.

Becomingly eminent, Tweed was once dubbed 'the British Rodin'. He trained, incidentally, with Hamo Thorneycroft, whose father Thomas made the Prince Consort statue in Halifax.

The rear of Cook's plinth depicts 'The Resolution' *("The ship of my choice… the fittest for service of any I have seen")*; is inscribed with noble sentiments ("To strive, to seek to find and not to yield"), and is bedizened with grateful plaques from the Caucasian 'inheritors' of far-flung continents.

Overseen by the mouldering jaw of a Right Whale, the punctilious navigator looks across the West Cliff towards distant copies of himself in Hawaii and Canada; still resplendent after his refurbishment in 2018 for the Cook 250 Festival. This is precisely what public sculpture is expected to be… but these days, rarely is.

The Sea Trek Sculpture on 'The Bull-nose" in Hull is obviously more intimate than the lofty Cook and is positioned in the modern, asymmetrical fashion which feigns informality. Yet it is, clearly, a conservative piece that invokes the tradition of public statuary that John Tweed embodied.

The constrainedly theatrical work is promoted as a memorial to over two million emigrants who travelled from Central Europe to America between 1836 and 1913. Its plinth makes specific reference to their journey via Hull's Paragon Train Station to Liverpool – where an identical statue is to be found.

In fact, there are identical statues in Oslo, Hamburg, Glasgow and Portsmouth – and while their associated scripts might be variously changed the intent by their donor remains; namely to celebrate the journey to Utah made by converts to the Church of Latter-day Saints. The Mormon newsletter of 2001 confidently advises its readers that each sculpture will bear a text that reads: *"I believed in the principle of the gathering and felt it my duty to go, although it was a severe trial to me in my feelings to leave my native land… But my heart was fixed. I knew in whom I had trusted, and with the true fire of Israel's God burning in my bosom, I forsook my home"*[1].

Except the sculpture in Hull doesn't say this. It not only has an inscribed solecism (which speaks of the 'Sea Trek Foundation'

THE SEA TREK SCULPTURE • HULL

THE LOST TRAWLERMEN • HULL

tracing their 'descendants journey' when it means their "ancestors' journey") but it is presently and unfortunately 'tagged'.

The Lost Trawlermen sculpture, by contrast, is anything but an imported product. It's the realisation of a long-cherished scheme to raise a permanent monument to the estimated 6,000 Hull trawlermen to have been lost at sea.

After over a decade of fund-raising and planning disappointments, the public was invited to choose a design and opted for Peter Naylor's group of silhouetted, weathered steel figures. Although laid out and duly blessed by the Archbishop of York, the figures still await the completion of a

'Garden of Social History' which has been delayed until 2020 by an integrated flood alleviation scheme.

The real issue, however, lies less with the delays than with the artistic quality of the piece. Will its blatantly photographic appeal endure? Viewed to seaward it perhaps has a graveyard resonance; but the reverse view (an intended aspect of the design) to the trite commercialism of St Andrews Retail Park is desperately disheartening.

It's a question to be answered individually. As the artist Richard Wilson remarked in a notable speech on the topic of public sculpture[2]: **"It allows us, as spectators, to take a position so we can let others know who we are or where we stand"**.

'James Cook RN', explorer (1728–1779) • Sculpted by John Tweed (1869–1933)

Notes

Introduction

1. https://www.royalacademy.org.uk/art-artists/name/michael-sandle-ra
2. https://en.wikipedia.org/wiki/7000_Oaks
3. https://public-art.shu.ac.uk/sheffield/index.html
If you prefer books, hunt out 'Public Sculpture of Sheffield and South Yorkshire' by Darcy White and Elizabeth Norman (Liverpool University Press). It costs more than the Internet, of course.
4. Although even this cursory scamper has not been a cheap exercise and I doubt that there will be a 'next time'.
5. https://en.wikipedia.org/wiki/Moses_(Michelangelo)
6. http://www.secretleeds.com/viewtopic.php?t=2784
7. Every time I go through Trafalgar Square I pledge to finally find out who General Napier actually is. I never do. I never will.
8. Except to point out that some of the smaller pictures in the book were taken with a ten year old pocket Ricoh GX100.

Boroughbridge Devil's Arrows

1. Richard Frank writing in 1694. Most of this information is on the web in various forms. Two comprehensive sites might be: https://historicengland.org.uk/listing/the-list/list-entry/1014705 and https://brigantesnation.com/devils-arrows-north-yorkshire
2. At least one writer - Hazel Wheeler in The Milliner's Apprentice: Girlhood in Edwardian Yorkshire attributes the bridge to John Metcalfe but the dates don't seem to tally.
3. The fact that there were certainly more than three stones dates these 'alternative names' to a more modern era.
4. Which isn't *quite* as picturesque as Turner's 1797 painting at Harewood House suggests...

Halifax Prince Consort

1. http://www.historywebsite.co.uk/listed/princealbert.htm
2. Web image from: http://1.bp.blogspot.com/-DGisDrlS67E/U5gqfeFnyWI/AAAAAAAABBE/jSCTMZ6neRI/s1600/SAM_0028.JPG
3. Web image from: http://www.victorianweb.org/sculpture/thornycroftt/4.html
4. Cavanagh, Terry. Public Sculpture of Liverpool. Liverpool: Liverpool University Press, 1996.

Hull King Billy

1. "To the gentleman in black velvet..."

Otley Thomas Chippendale

1. £20 note from 1970–91.
2. To be fair, a claim can be made for the authenticity of the Chandos portrait of Shakespeare.
3. Sam Chippindale (1909–1990), has an obtuse sundial erected to his memory in Tittybottle Park *(picture above)* which describes him as a 'pioneer, genius and legend'. He was an Otley estate agent who in the 1960's jointly instigated the rash of Arndale Centres around the country.

Harewood Orpheus

1. Astrid Zydower - Her Life & Works by Peter C. Amsden
2. e.g. John Macallan Swan's 'Orpheus' in the Lady Lever Collection at Port Sunlight.
3. Rainer Maria Rilke: 'The Sonnets to Orpheus'
4. Sydney Goodsir Smith: 'Orpheus' from 'Under the Eildon Tree'.
 "My hert, a leopard, ruthless, breme,
 Gilravaged far and near
 Seekan sensatiouns, passions that wad wauken
 My Muse whan she was lollish."

Bradford Cromwell

1. Nearly all the UK statues of Cromwell are late Victorian, namely in London (1899), Manchester (1875), Warrington (1899) and St.Ives, Cambridge (1901). They were all controversial, principally due to Cromwell's harshly oppressive actions in Ireland.
2. Images of Oliver Cromwell by Roger Howell

York Constantine The Great

1. https://www.yorkpress.co.uk/news/16385787.mystery-of-the-missing-fingers-when-did-statue-of-artist-william-etty-lose-most-of-his-right-hand/?ref=rss
2. The three figures on Brixton station were regular commuters who volunteered themselves to Kevin Atherton. Two were black (Peter Lloyd and Joy Battick) and the third was German (Karin Heistermann). That their identities remain known makes them more potent than the generic figures used to assuage anxieties about elitism.

Pocklington Wilberforce

1. Glory and Bollocks: the truth behind ten defining events in British History by Colin Brown

Hull Voyage
1. https://www.visithull.org/discover/article/statue-stories-from-hull-to-iceland/
2. https://www.bbc.co.uk/news/uk-england-humber-14974892

Barnsley Dickie Bird
1. Brian Lewis (b. Birmingham 1937) is a Pontefract-based writer and artist. One of the few people with more opinions than the author; a statue in his honour is an inevitability.
2. https://www.dailymail.co.uk/news/article-2484131/Statue-cricket-umpire-Dickie-Bird-lifted-feet-stop-drunk-revellers-hanging-knickers-bras-famous-raised-finger.html

Barnsley Joseph Locke
1. Much of this information comes from Wikipedia, which the author fiscally supports and salutes.
2. It should be mentioned that Julian Barnes fictionalised the building of Barentin Viaduct in his 1996 short story collection 'Cross Channel'; but thenagain he's a pretentious twat who gets too much attention as it is.
3. If you are, indeed, keen on statues and have not come across René & Peter van der Krogt

(who took the picture in Barentin) then you must visit their website: http://statues.vanderkrogt.net.

Darlington Train
1. https://www.thenorthernecho.co.uk/history/15365562.the-20th-anniversary-of-darlingtons-controversial-brick-train-sculpture/
2. https://www.steveniceton.co.uk/the-seated-man-castleton-rigg/ [This, erm, challenging piece vanished before we visited the East Coast and was last seen - somewhat unexpectedly - en route to the West Yorkshire Sculpture Park.

Leeds Brick Man
1. Consider this example... https://www.yorkshire-post.co.uk/news/where-to-now-for-cultural-soul-of-leeds-1-2494077

Morley Ernie Wise
1. http://news.bbc.co.uk/1/hi/england/west_yorkshire/8549577.stm

Huddersfield Harold Wilson
1. Keith Flett: https://kmflett.wordpress.com/2018/06/07/mary-wilson-the-huddersfield-statue-the-pipe/

Sheffield Women of Steel
1. https://en.wikipedia.org/wiki/James_Montgomery_(poet)
I could happily have written about Montgomery at length. His 'redemption' contrasts markedly with the fate of the Rigg Family Monument in York to which he lent his pen (http://yorkstories.co.uk/memorials/a-forgotten-tragedy-rigg-family-monument/).
2. https://www.thestar.co.uk/news/unveiled-sheffields-brave-women-of-steel-honoured-with-statue-61108
3. https://en.wikipedia.org/wiki/Man_of_Steel_(sculpture)

Rudston Monument
1. No marksman, Old Nick at least got closer to St. Mary's Church than he did to Aldborough with the Devil's Arrows.

Otley Bull Stone
1. https://megalithix.wordpress.com/2009/12/22/bull-stone-guiseley/

Doncaster The Lovers
1. http://www.danceshistoricalmiscellany.com/russias-dumping-grounds-for-soviet-sculpture/
2. https://www.telegraph.co.uk/news/worldnews/asia/india/1504473/Rescuing-the-Raj.html
3. https://www.sheffieldtelegraph.co.uk/news/designer-of-saucy-doncaster-statue-sees-artwork-for-first-time-ever-61710

Sheffield Walking Man
1. From Sculpture in the Garden ed. Patrick Eyres (publ. Routledge 2017)
2. Sculpture and Survival, Serpentine Gallery, London, op.cit, p.9
3. https://public-art.shu.ac.uk/sheffield/full30.html

Filey – A High Tide in Short Wellies
1. In 2013 Maureen bought a third Lonsdale sculpture for the East Coast that depicts a Tunny Fish being landed and which is sited near the Marine Drive Toll House. Its pointy tale led to 'Health and Safety' misgivings and – perhaps in a bid to stall her serial philanthropy – Scarborough Council gently advised Maureen that they would need to "review and develop a forward plan for siting additional public art in the borough". https://

Foot Notes

www.thescarboroughnews.co.uk/news/wonderful-tunny-fish-sculpture-is-finally-unveiled-on-east-pier-1-5874532

2. 'A high tide in short wellies' :–
   That's it for me, I'll see you later.
   Gonna wrap this catch in protective paper,
   Gonna face the sea with a thousand mile stare
   And wish that I was floating there
   In its summertime.
   Down on the pier I saw a man with a board
   It read 'the end is near, accept your lord".
   Then underneath this some fisherman wrote.
   'I can see the end from the back of my boat'
   This is wintertime.
3. Scarborough News, 12 Oct 2017

Market Weighton William Bradley
1. http://providerfiles.thedms.co.uk/eandamedia/YS/2170245_1.pdf
2. https://en.wikipedia.org/wiki/Cigar_store_Indian

Bridlington Gansey Girl
1. https://www.youtube.com/watch?v=B4gv3q-JQT80

2. http://www.sutcliffe-gallery.co.uk/_photo_3200049.html
3. https://www.bridlingtonfreepress.co.uk/business/in-pictures-bridlington-s-gansey-girl-1-7604704
4. Tee Shirt - https://fineartamerica.com/featured/the-gansey-girl-by-steve-carvill-david-hollingworth.html?product=adult-tshirt
5. https://www.bridlingtonfreepress.co.uk/news/people/the-secret-sculpture-what-is-coming-to-bridlington-s-seafront-1-9843338
6. https://www.galleryforty-nine.com/stephen-carvill

Reighton Shepherd and Sheep
1. http://www.ronaldfalck-artist.co.uk/viewpoints.html

Whitby James Cook RN *et al.*.
1. http://rhaworth.me/se/stf_lds.htm
2. https://3rd-dimensionpmsa.org.uk/pmsa-news/2017-11-12-pmsas-marsh-awards-2017-richard-wilson-ra